PRESENTED BY **UNIQVISE** INSIGHTFUL BOOKS

ASTROPHYSICS FOR YOUR LITTLE ONE

Minutely illustrated journey of A Baby, Riley! With Plenty of Parent Notes!

FOR BUSINESS ENQUIRIES EMAIL AT: "UNIQVISE@GMAIL.COM"

Hello and welcome to the Universe! The Universe is

Reading time

everything around us, filled with stars, planets, and galaxies. It's like a giant puzzle waiting for us to explore.

This is my new Astro-bracelet, isn't it cute!

Riley: Look at all these stars! They're like big glowing lights in the sky, each one a home to planets and moons! Do you think there are aliens living on those planets?

PARENT NOTE -

Universe: Everything that exists, including stars, planets, and galaxies.
Galaxies: Huge star clusters in space.
Space: The big, empty area where stars and planets are.

Stars are giant balls of hot, glowing gases. They make their own light and heat. The Sun is a star, and it's the closest star to Earth.

Imagine flying close to a star!

Riley: Stars are so bright because they have a lot of energy inside them. Some stars are much bigger and hotter than the Sun, and they shine like cosmic beacons in the night sky!

PARENT NOTE

Stars: Giant balls of hot gas that shine in the sky.

Think NEXT

WHY DO STARS LOOK POINTY?

UNREAL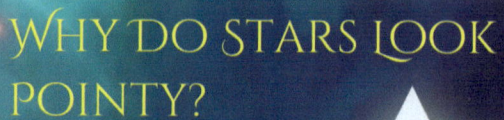

Answer: Stars often look like they have five points because that's how people usually draw them. But guess what? Stars are actually round!

REAL

WHY DO THEY LOOK POINTY THEN?

Answer: It's because of how light bends when it hits objects, making stars look like they have rays.

Planets are big balls that go around stars, just like Earth goes around the Sun. Some planets are rocky, like Earth and Mars, while others are made of gas, like Jupiter and Saturn.

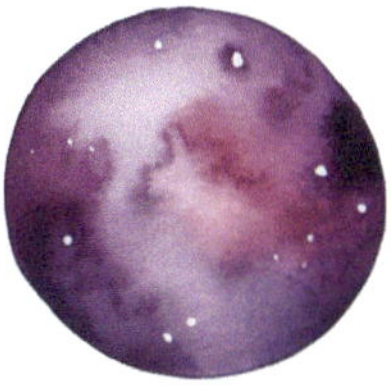

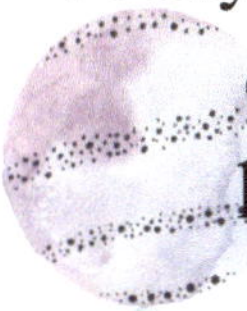

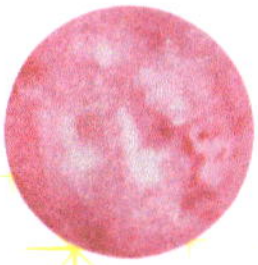

Which planet would you like to visit?

Riley: Earth is a rocky planet, and it's our home! It has oceans, mountains, and lots of living things, like us!

Other planets in our solar system are very different. Some are cold, some are hot, and some have big storms!

Gravity is a force that pulls things toward the center of planets and stars. It's what keeps us on the ground and makes things fall down.

Riley: Gravity is like a big invisible hand that holds everything on Earth. It's why we don't float away when we jump!

What if there was no gravity? We could jump really high!

PARENT NOTE -
Gravity: Pulls things down to the ground. It's what keeps us on Earth.

If you had a moon, what would you name it?

Moons are natural satellites that orbit planets. They don't make their own light but shine because of the light from their star.

— & —

bestie

Riley: Our Moon is Earth's best friend in space! Some planets have many moons, while others have none at all! It lights up the night sky and changes shape as it moves around us like new moon, crescent moon, gibbous moon, and full moon.

PARENT NOTE -

Moons: Natural satellites that orbit planets. Earth's moon is a famous one!

Galaxies are enormous collections of stars, gas, and dust held together by gravity. Our galaxy, the Milky Way, is shaped like a spiral.

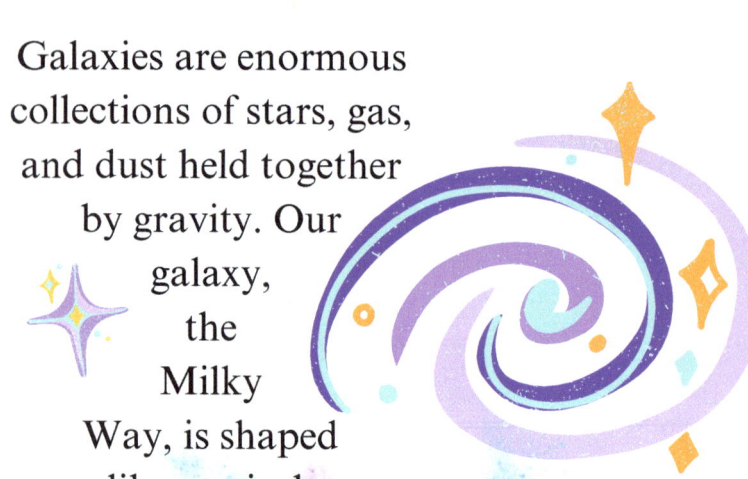

If you could visit a galaxy, which one would you choose?

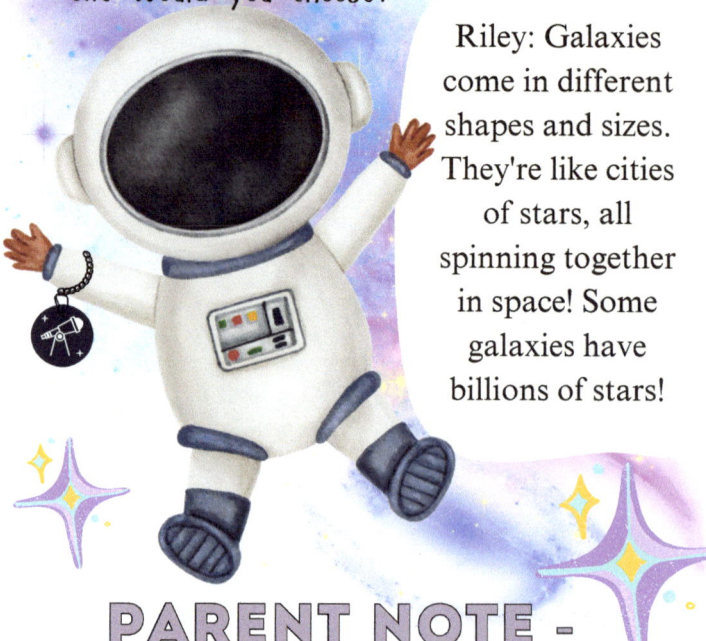

Riley: Galaxies come in different shapes and sizes. They're like cities of stars, all spinning together in space! Some galaxies have billions of stars!

PARENT NOTE -

Galaxies: Enormous collections of stars, gas, and dust. Our Milky Way is one of them.

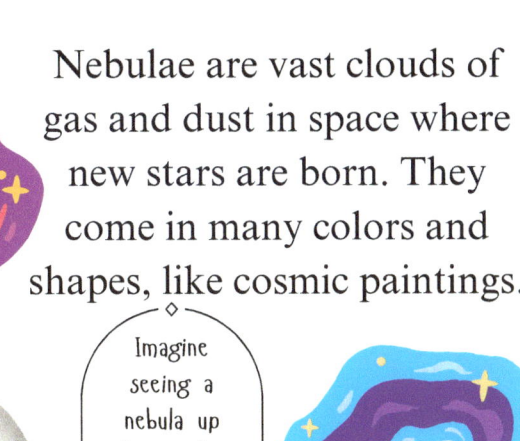

Nebulae are vast clouds of gas and dust in space where new stars are born. They come in many colors and shapes, like cosmic paintings.

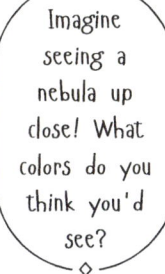

Imagine seeing a nebula up close! What colors do you think you'd see?

Riley: Nebulae are like space nurseries where baby stars are born!

They're also where planets begin to form, surrounded by swirling gases and dust.

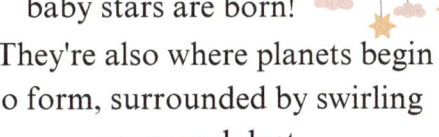

PARENT NOTE -

Nebulae: Vast clouds of gas and dust where new stars are born.

Black holes are incredibly dense objects with gravity so strong that nothing, not even light, can escape them. They form when massive stars collapse.

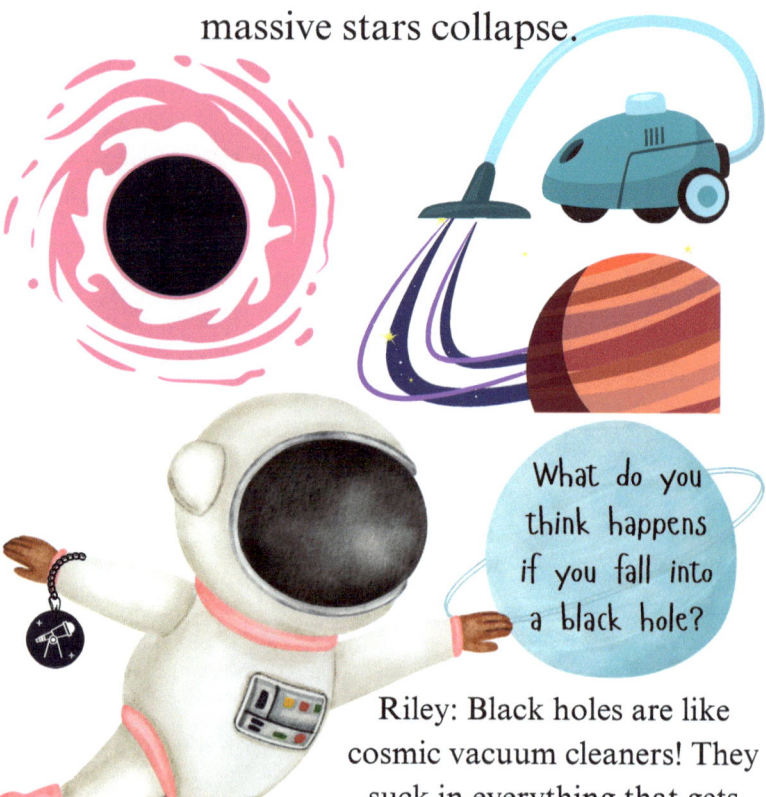

What do you think happens if you fall into a black hole?

Riley: Black holes are like cosmic vacuum cleaners! They suck in everything that gets too close to them. They're some of the most mysterious things in the Universe!

PARENT NOTE -

Black Holes: Incredibly dense objects with strong gravity that pulls everything in.

Supernovae are explosive events that occur when massive stars reach the end of their lives. They shine incredibly brightly and spread elements like stardust across space.

Riley: When a star explodes as a supernova, it's like fireworks in space! It's a dramatic way for stars to end their lives and send their materials back into the Universe.

If you could see a supernova from Earth, what do you think it would look like?

PARENT NOTE -

Supernovae: Explosive events when massive stars reach the end of their lives.

Comets are icy objects that come from the outer edges of the solar system. When they get closer to the Sun, they develop glowing tails of gas and dust.

If you could ride a comet, where would you go?

Riley: Comets are like cosmic snowballs with long, bright tails! They come from really far away and bring us beautiful shows in the night sky.

PARENT NOTE -

Comets: Icy objects from the outer solar system with glowing tails.

Asteroids are rocky objects that orbit the Sun, mostly found in the asteroid belt between Mars and Jupiter. They are leftovers from the early days of our solar system.

MARS

JUPITER

Riley: Asteroids are like space rocks that travel around the Sun. Sometimes they bump into each other and create shooting stars!

What do you think asteroids are made of?

PARENT NOTE -

Asteroids: Rocky objects that orbit the Sun, leftovers from the formation of our solar system.

ASTEROIDS ARE DIFFERENT FROM COMETS

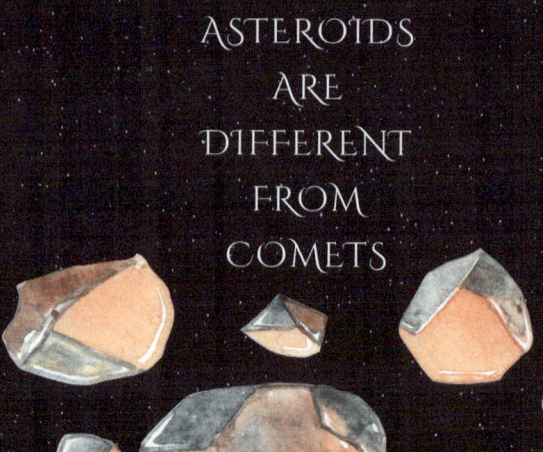

Hey! Did you know asteroids and comets are like space cousins, but they're actually quite different? Asteroids are like big rocky space rocks, kind of like the

rocks you find in your backyard. But comets are icy and have long tails that glow when they get close to the Sun, like a comet wearing a shiny cape! Isn't it cool how different things can be in space?

But comets are icy and have long tails that glow when they get close to the Sun, like a comet wearing a shiny cape! Isn't it cool how different things can be in space?

Telescopes are tools that help us see far into space by collecting light from distant objects. They come in different sizes and can be on Earth or in space.

Riley: Telescopes are like giant eyes that scientists use to study stars, planets, and galaxies. They help us learn more about the Universe!

If you had a telescope, what would you want to look at?

EARTH TELESCOPE

SPACE TELESCOPE

PARENT NOTE -

Telescopes: Tools that collect light from distant objects to help us see them clearly.

Light years measure the distance that light travels in one year, which is about 6 trillion miles! It helps us understand how far things are in space.

Riley: C for measuring how far stars and galaxies are from us. They tell us about the vastness of the Universe!

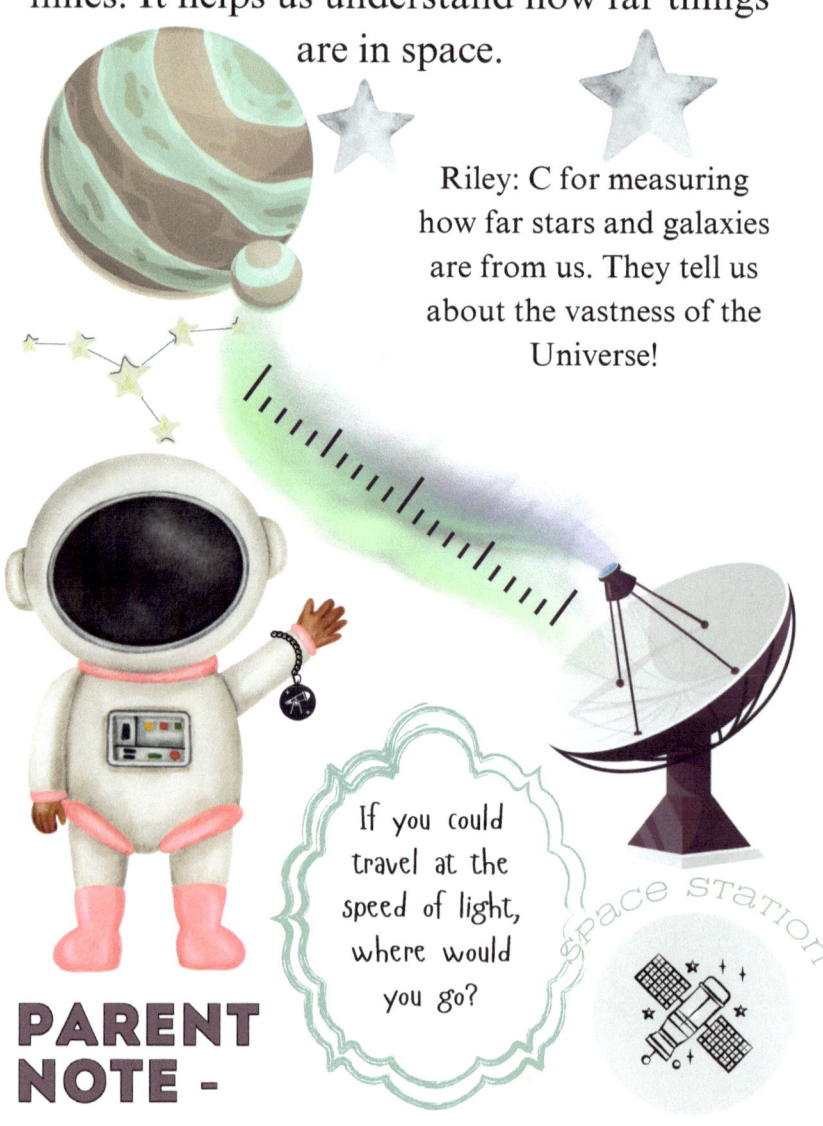

If you could travel at the speed of light, where would you go?

PARENT NOTE -

Light Years: Measure the distance that light travels in one year.

Exoplanets are planets that orbit stars outside our solar system. Scientists study them to learn more about the possibility of life beyond Earth.

EXOPLANET

STAR

If you could visit any exoplanet, which one would you choose?

Riley: Exoplanets are like distant cousins of Earth, orbiting other stars. Some might have oceans like ours, or even aliens living on them!

PARENT NOTE -

Exoplanets: Planets that orbit stars outside our solar system.

The Big Bang is the theory that explains how the Universe began billions of years ago from a single, incredibly hot and dense point. It started everything we see today.

Riley: The Big Bang is like the ultimate fireworks show that created everything in the Universe! It's amazing to think about how everything started from one tiny point.

What do you think came before the Big Bang?

BIG BANG

HOT POINT

PARENT NOTE -

Big Bang: The theory that explains the beginning of the Universe.

Stars have a life cycle, starting from birth in nebulae, shining brightly in their middle age, and eventually ending in dramatic events like supernovae or becoming white dwarfs.

NEBULA

Riley: Stars are like cosmic storytellers with a beginning, middle, and end! Some stars live fast and explode, while others fade away quietly.

PROTOSTAR

If you were a star, how would you want your story to end?

SUPERNOVA

PARENT NOTE -

Star Life Cycle: Stages stars go through from birth to death.

STAR LIFE CYCLE

Nebula Formation

Protostar Formation

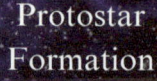

Main Sequence Star

Red Supernova

OOPS! THAT'S HOW YOU SEE! BUT, REMEMBER REALITY IS ROUND.

Space exploration is the journey of humans and robots into outer space to discover more about the Universe, planets, and the possibility of life beyond Earth.

If you could explore anywhere in space, where would you go first?

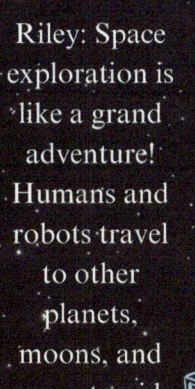

Riley: Space exploration is like a grand adventure! Humans and robots travel to other planets, moons, and even asteroids.

PARENT NOTE -

Space Exploration: Journey into outer space to learn about the Universe.

NOTE TO PARENT/GUARDIAN:

Introducing your little one to the wonders of astrophysics might seem like a daunting task, but if you're holding this book, it means you have extraordinary aspirations for your child. You're setting the stage for a future scientist, an explorer of the cosmos! Imagine granting your child the freedom to envision a cat in a space suit, visiting planets and journeying through the stars. Such imaginative play is the bedrock of learning and discovery. By nurturing this sense of wonder, you're fostering a free mind that can dream big and think beyond the ordinary. Astrophysics is a gateway to endless curiosity and cognitive development. By immersing your child in the awe-inspiring concepts of our universe, you're not only stimulating their young minds but also igniting a lifelong passion for discovery. Whether it's marveling at the stars, understanding the vastness of space, or pondering the mysteries of black holes, every lesson is a step toward a future filled with exploration and innovation. So, don't stop here! Keep nurturing that spark of curiosity. Share the examples in this book, come up with your own creative ways to explain the wonders of the universe, and revisit these concepts often. The more exposure your child gets, the more their imagination will flourish. Who knows? Your child might one day be among the great minds unraveling the secrets of the cosmos. Keep up the extraordinary parenting drive, and watch your little one reach for the stars!

BY SADAF SHAHAB AZMI, FOUNDER [UNIQVISE]

from the bottom of my heart, Thank you!

UNIQVISE

is my initiative to spread
authentic and simplified
information in an unique and to
the point talks. I am an
university student and looking
forward to change myself and
elevate the condition of current
chaotic world with the help of the
Creator, the one! Catch me at
instagram account: "UNIQVISE".

FOR BUSINESS ENQUIRIES EMAIL AT: "UNIQVISE@GMAIL.COM"

CUT OUT THIS CERTIFICATE AND
DECOR YOUR CHAMP ROOM!

MINI DIPLOMA IN ASTROPHYSICS

This certifies that

----

has ventured into the fascinating world of Astrophysics! For your Astronomical leaps and bounds in early learning!

FOR CURIOUS MINDS THAT REACH FOR THE STARS AND ASK 'WHAT IF?'

DATE OF ISSUANCE:

WRITE ABOVE BABY'S NAME & DAY YOU REACHED HERE!

CUT OUT THIS CERTIFICATE AND
DECOR YOUR CHAMP ROOM!

www.ingramcontent.com/pod-product-compliance
Lightning Source LLC
Chambersburg PA
CBHW041512010526
44118CB00006B/230